KRUPP DIGGING MACHINE

BY QUINN M. ARNOLD

CREATIVE EDUCATION • CREATIVE PAPERBACKS

Published by Creative Education and Creative Paperbacks
P.O. Box 227, Mankato, Minnesota 56002
Creative Education and Creative Paperbacks are imprints
of The Creative Company
www.thecreativecompany.us

Design by The Design Lab
Production by Chelsey Luther
Art direction by Rita Marshall
Printed in the United States of America

Photographs by Alamy (Agencja Fotograficzna Caro,
imageBROKER, Bernd Lauter), Corbis (Science Photo Library),
Dreamstime (Mikhail Lavrenov), Getty Images (Images Etc Ltd),
Newscom (Federico Gambarini/dpa/picture-alliance, Ingram
Publishing), Shutterstock (corlaffra)

Library of Congress Cataloging-in-Publication Data
Arnold, Quinn M.
Krupp digging machine / by Quinn M. Arnold.
p. cm. – (Now that's big!)
Includes bibliographical references and index.
Summary: A high-interest introduction to the size, speed, and
purpose of one of the world's largest excavators, including a brief
history and what the future holds for the Krupp Digging Machine.

ISBN 978-1-60818-713-3 (hardcover)
ISBN 978-1-62832-309-2 (pbk)
ISBN 978-1-56660-749-0 (eBook)
1. Excavating machinery—Juvenile literature. 2. Coal-mining
machinery—Juvenile literature.

TA735.A68 2016
621.8/65—dc23   2015045207

CCSS: RI.1.1, 2, 3, 4, 5, 6, 7; RI.2.1, 2, 4, 5, 6, 7, 10; RF.1.1, 3, 4;
RF.2.3, 4

First Edition HC 9 8 7 6 5 4 3 2 1
First Edition PBK 9 8 7 6 5 4 3 2 1

TABLE OF CONTENTS

4

What are the biggest vehicles on Earth? Bucket wheel excavators are giant digging machines. One of the biggest is the Bagger 288. It weighs 14,880 tons (13,500 t).

The Bagger 288 is two football fields long.

Bucket wheel excavators are used in open-pit mines. They dig up overburden. The Bagger 288 can dig down 328 feet (100 m). It is as tall as 17 giraffes stacked on top of each other.

Germany has some of the world's largest coal mines.

ThyssenKrupp has made many big digging machines. Their diggers are used in mines around the world. Krupp finished the Bagger 288 in 1978. It works in German coal mines.

The treads are taller than professional basketball players.

tank treads

The Bagger 288 is powered by electricity. It has 12 tank treads. Each tread is 12 feet (3.7 m) wide and 46 feet (14 m) around. The treads help the machine move over uneven land.

The Bagger 288 took 3 weeks to move 14 miles (22.5 km).

The Bagger 288 worked in a mine for 23 years. In 2001, it went to a different mine. It took a long time to get there. A tortoise is faster than the Bagger 288!

Once, the Bagger 288 scooped up a bulldozer by mistake.

The digging wheel is more than 70 feet (21.3 m) tall. It has 18 buckets. Each bucket can hold 233 cubic feet (6.6 cu m) of overburden. That's 1,743 gallons per scoop!

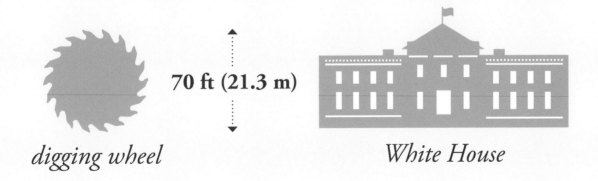

digging wheel   70 ft (21.3 m)   White House

A five-person crew runs the Bagger 288.

The Bagger 288 never stops working. It can fill more than 2,500 dump trucks with overburden every day.

Power stations near coal mines turn the coal into energy.

A bigger digging machine was built in 1995. But it cannot move more overburden than the Bagger 288. ThyssenKrupp's biggest digging machine will keep working for a long time.

1995

HOW BIG

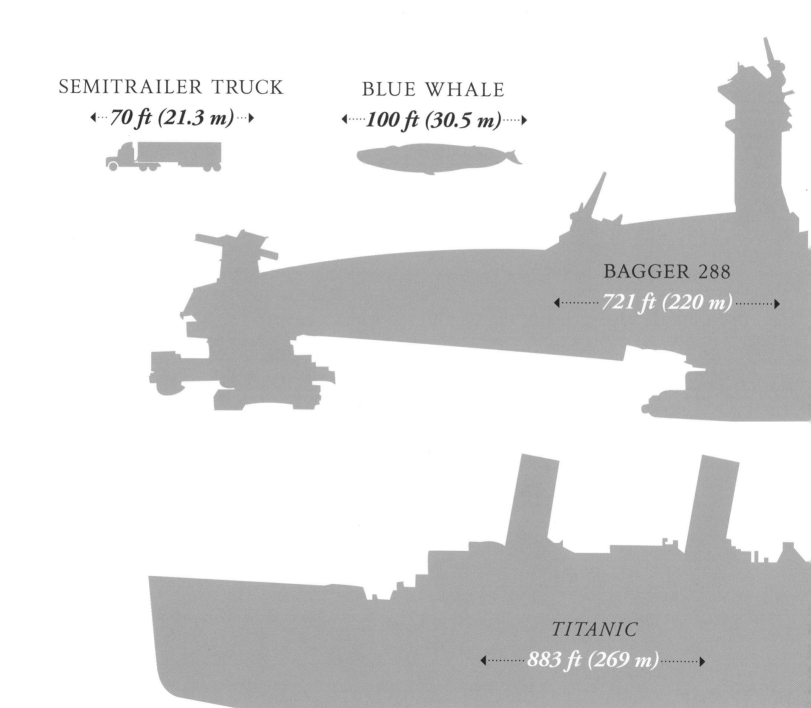

SEMITRAILER TRUCK
◄····· *70 ft (21.3 m)* ····►

BLUE WHALE
◄····· *100 ft (30.5 m)* ····►

BAGGER 288
◄····· *721 ft (220 m)* ·····►

TITANIC
◄····· *883 ft (269 m)* ·····►

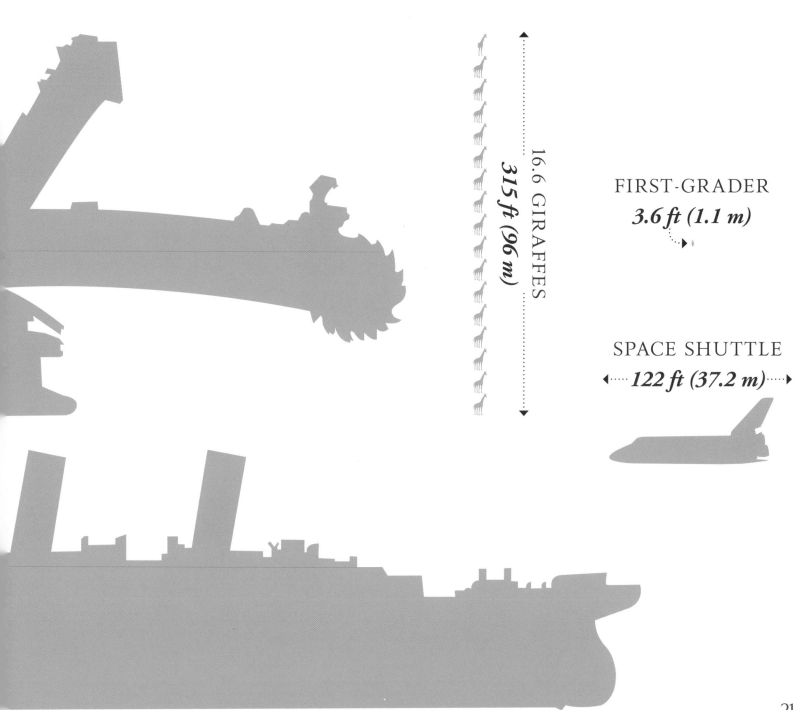

16.6 GIRAFFES
315 ft (96 m)

FIRST-GRADER
3.6 ft (1.1 m)

SPACE SHUTTLE
◄···· **122 ft (37.2 m)** ····►

21

GLOSSARY

bucket wheel excavators—*machines used in open-pit mines to dig down to an underground store of minerals*

open-pit mines—*mines where machines dig into the ground from the surface*

overburden—*the soil, rocks, and other materials above an underground store of minerals, such as coal*

tank treads—*metal bands looped around the wheels of heavy vehicles to help them move*

READ MORE

Gilbert, Sara. *Diggers.*
Mankato, Minn.: Creative Education, 2009.

Gordon, Nick. *Monster Diggers.*
Minneapolis: Bellwether Media, 2014.

WEBSITES

Energy Kids: Nonrenewable Coal
http://www.eia.gov/kids/energy.cfm?page=coal_home-basics
Learn all about how coal is formed, the different types of coal, and coal mining.

Energy Star Kids
http://www.energystar.gov/index.cfm?c=kids.kids_index
Learn more about different types of energy, where it comes from, and how you can save energy each day.

INDEX